An Introduction to

Transformative Tarot Counseling

The High Art of Reading

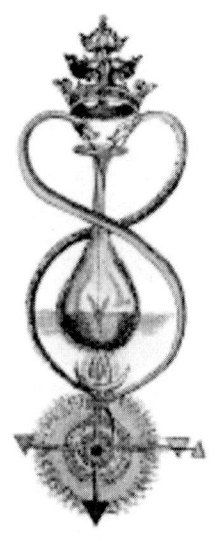

KATRINA WYNNE, M.A.

An Introduction to
Transformative Tarot Counseling
The High Art of Reading

A *Sacred Rose Publishing* book

First Edition Copyright © 2012 by Katrina Wynne.

Requests for permission should be addressed to:

Sacred Rose Publishing
c/o Katrina Wynne
P.O. Box 956
Yachats, OR 97498-0956
E-mail: mail@katrinawynne.org

ISBN 978-1-937493-09-7 (paperback)
ISBN 978-1-937493-10-3 (e-book)
  1. Tarot-Psychological aspects. I. Title
Library of Congress Control Number: 2012936307

Editors: Jaymi Elford & Thomas Anderson
Cover and Interior Design: Katrina Wynne
Cover Art: Qahira Lynn / www.qahiralynn.com
Printer: Rose at Lazerquick, Newport, OR, USA

Illustrations from *Voyager Tarot* deck reproduced by permission of James Wanless / Merrill-West Publishing, Carmel, CA, USA.
Copyright © 1984 by Merrill-West Publishing

Note: This publication contains the opinions and ideas of its author. It is intended to provide helpful and informative material on the subject matter covered. It is sold with the understanding that the author /publisher are not engaged in rendering professional services in the book. If the reader requires personal assistance or advice, a competent professional should be consulted.

The author/publisher specifically disclaim any responsibility for any liability, loss or risk, personal or otherwise, which is incurred as a consequence, directly or indirectly, of the use and application of any of the contents of this book.

For all those who love Tarot

and desire to live

its wisdom.

To Ethony

—In Light
And Love —
♡ Katrina
RS19

Contents

Preface

How does one find words to describe the un-describable aspects of Tarot work in a comprehensive manner? This challenge impeded my willingness to write about my experience and wisdom with Tarot for many years. After much meditation and consulting the cards for guidance, a solution emerged, to simplify the breadth of this first offering on the subject of Transformative Tarot Counseling™ (TTC), allowing it to initiate interested readers with the basic concepts of this approach to reading Tarot for oneself or others. As an introduction to TTC, the depth of material and experience-oriented style of my work cannot be totally expressed in words or examples.

Much like Tarot, the real message and meaning is in your relationship to the Tarot, either by studying it as a book of wisdom, or through your experience working with the cards. In this case, TTC is an awareness exercise and skill set aimed at raising the bar on your relationship with the Tarot, your clients, and especially yourself. TTC emphasizes the importance of counseling skills and your presence as a guide when you read for yourself or others.

This book is an introduction to highly developed and interactive skills that Tarot consultants can apply to their readings. Throughout the book I use the term "querent" to represent the person consulting the cards, which includes self-reading. For interactive readings between two people, I use the terms "reader," the person offering the reading and "client," the person receiving the reading.

Skills for All Reading Modalities

Although Tarot reading is the focus of this work, the concepts can be applied to all metaphysical consultations (astrology, palmistry, numerology, oracle, etc.), with special emphasis on the techniques in the chapters on counseling skills and ethics.

Acknowledgements

My journey with Tarot began around 1972, but it wasn't until 1988 when I began my studies in Process-Oriented Psychology, developed by Dr. Arnold Mindell, that my Transformative Tarot Counseling™ style emerged. I wish to thank Amy and Arny Mindell and the Process Work community for their ongoing enrichment of my psychotherapeutic skills.

The internet is teaming with Tarot writers, weblogs, and social networking communities. Appreciation goes to all the creative souls in cyberspace for inspiring me and sharing in occasional exchanges on our favorite topic.

Special recognition goes to the many Tarot Meetup groups and Tarot organizations, such as the American Tarot Association and the San Francisco Bay Area Tarot Symposium, who have hosted my various Tarot talks.

Editors extraordinaire, Jaymi Elford and Thomas Anderson make me sound more better. Thanks! Qahira Lynn is the amazing visionary artist who has taken my vision and painted it into life. Big thanks to James Wanless for gracious use of his *Voyager Tarot* cards. Much appreciation is extended to Rose at Newport Lazerquick for holding my hand through the printing process and to Carla Perry of Dancing Moon Press for her expert advice for publishing.

Finally, I wish to express my greatest appreciation for your interest in learning more about the power of Tarot.

1

What is Transformative Tarot Counseling?

"Having responded to his own call, and continuing to follow courageously as the consequences unfold, the hero finds all the forces of the unconscious at his side... the soul under the tutelage of the supernatural."
— Joseph Campbell

Transformative Tarot Counseling™ (TTC) is the high art of reading cards for yourself or others.

"Transformative" — allowing change to emerge. It is the process by which *magic* can occur. Magic is the art of changing from one form to another, moving from the known through the unknown, bringing the unconscious to light.

"Counseling" — the practice of interacting with others in an affirming and supportive way. The skills utilized in this style of working with Tarot reading respects the client's wisdom, and boundaries, allowing a deeper experience of the cards.

This transformative style with Tarot has evolved based on my work as a professional counselor with sound ethical values for honoring my client's life, personal power, and process. My training in psychotherapy has taught me dynamic and meaningful ways to work with Tarot clients, tapping their magical process as we reveal the core of their being. This is the heart of what is taught through my *Transformative Tarot Counseling™ Certification Program*. You can read more information about this program on my website: TarotCounseling.org

Change toward transformation is the most essential message and method of Tarot. We evolve as living beings learning life's lessons as we move through time. In order to raise our awareness and receive the Tarot's guidance for this journey, it helps to go beyond what we already know about the Tarot cards. With this approach even the act of reading Tarot cards is potentially transformative for the reader.

Counseling Insights in Tarot Readings

If you have experienced counseling or are trained in counseling skills you may know that the job of a counselor is not to give simple advice or direct clients on what to do, but rather, to assist clients in uncovering issues and support them in finding their personal power and wholeness. For example, if a counselor told the client in the middle of discussing a work issue, "Just quit your job!" in most cases the client would resist this directive. It just isn't useful information. If it were that easy, the client would not have come in for counseling in the first place. There is always more to the story than what meets the surface. Directives and predictions do not support clients in discovering and choosing changes they may need to make, or in empowering personal decision-making. In most cases, it only scratches the surface of the story.

Rather than reporting an interpretation of the cards in the layout for the client, a technique that tends to feed the mind, the client and reader engage their attention of the cards while the client discovers more personally derived meaning and heartfelt guidance. By noting the words, feelings, and insights of the client, associations are discovered, connections are made, and a deeper story begins to unveil.

Insight *and* integration are the goals of TTC, for which *experience* is a necessary bridge. To experience the energy of the cards brings them to life, while also feeding one's awareness.

How can I support what is most alive in you? This is the question that goes through my mind and heart as I work with clients and students using counseling or Tarot. I have no interest in predicting the future or telling people what decision to make. I believe that disempowers clients and their relationship to their life's journey. I'm looking for guidance that comes from the clients, through their awareness, conscious or subconscious, which knows where they are on their journey and what step is next.

Nonetheless, I believe there is a reading style and reader for everyone. All styles have their place in the world. My unique offering to clients and students through TTC is a more interactive way of looking at the relationship between clients, cards, and their guidance.

One of the main contrasts between counseling and predictive styles of reading is whether the reading is "descriptive" or "prescriptive." Like it sounds, a prescriptive reading occurs when Tarot readers report their interpretation of the cards and prescribe a particular meaning or action. For example, if VII Chariot appears in the reading, the assumption may be "you will be moving."

Descriptive readers share or reveal information based on the cards, without imposing their personal interpretation of what it means to the client. Ultimately, only the client can determine how useful the information is and how to apply it. More information about the counseling style of reading will be explained in Chapter 4 of this book.

Following the Client

Another dimension in TTC involves "following" versus "leading" the client. Following clients in Tarot reading is more challenging for readers to grasp. It is easy to lead the client with your interpretation of the cards and what you think they mean as the client follows your advice, interpretation, or guidance.

I believe one of the greatest gifts of studying and using Tarot cards is developing one's intuition and ability to grow closer to Source. How one uses the information gathered, especially in relationship to others, is where I become concerned. It can be empowering for the reader as they dazzle the client with their psychic ability, but that risks leaving behind the client's insight and bond with their own material.

A more challenging approach involves listening to or "following" the client, engaging them in the reading process, inviting the client to open to their own intuitive relationship with the cards, and then supporting them in discovering their own solution, action, meaning. The reader takes a back seat to the client and their cards, while allowing the client's wisdom to shine on their own with the reader's experienced guidance in the process. This also means the client works more in the reading and is not a passive recipient. This may not be the most popular position for those clients hoping to transfer responsibility for their decisions or actions to some third party, such as the reader.

What might this look like in a reading? It can be as simple as turning a card face up and asking the client about their "first impression." Most readers immediately jump in with an interpretation of the card, drowning out the initial glimmer of curiosity and connection from the client.

Typical readings feed the intellect, an experience from the neck up, but do not necessarily touch one's body-mind-emotion-soul. The goal of a *Transformative Tarot Counselor*™ is to provide a safe and professional environment to afford the client the opportunity to go as deeply into their process as they choose to proceed, within the "scope of practice" of the reader.

Transformative Tarot Counseling™ is not meant to replace a professional counseling session. Yet, it approaches the client with the same degree of respect for the complexity of life issues and spiritual concerns. All professionals are trained to know when an issue is beyond their scope of practice, and they are prepared to make referrals to qualified resources. This is also emphasized in the professional training involved with the Transformative Tarot Counseling™ Certification Program.

In the next chapter, we will look specifically at the potential and pattern for transformation and change within a Tarot reading

2

Tarot Magic and Change

"The only constant is change"
  — *I Ching - The Book of Changes*

Life *is* change, yet it is all too human to resist change and prefer the comfort of a predictable life. Many of us resist change and the work involved, even when that life is unhappy or painful. Sometimes we fear "rocking the boat" for others. We fall into known patterns of behavior with their associated pitfalls.

This chapter is dedicated to the idea of change, describing the necessary steps to transforming our lives and supporting new possibilities for our clients, then laying out these steps as they may appear in a Tarot session.

As Tarot consultants, we often hear the same concerns from clients: about relationships and love, career and money, health and wellbeing. Some clients return with repeating issues and we witness these issues cycling around again. This is clear evidence of old patterns active in their lives.

In my work as a Tarot reader I sometimes think of my service as "brief therapy," for it may be the first time someone has dared to examine an issue in the presence of a professional consultant. I wonder how many people are willing to contact a Tarot reader for guidance, but would never set foot in a counseling office. Whether you have training as a counselor or not, most readers are being called upon by clients to fulfill that role. For this reason I believe it is in our best interest as readers to learn more about counseling skills and ethics. Not to take the place of a professional counselor, but to understand the delicate role we occupy when serving the public, and to understand those limitations.

In Transformative Tarot Counseling™ (TTC), there is emphasis on understanding the reader's "scope-of-practice" — when to refer a client to an appropriate and effective healing or helping professional. Yet, there are useful skills and perspectives you can bring into your Tarot work that supports change and growth for clients. Chapter 4 introduces specific skills for Tarot readers to integrate into their work to be more effective. Chapter 5 covers ethical considerations for this profession.

The Art and Magic of Change

"Magic is a series of psychological techniques so devised
as to enable us to probe more deeply into ourselves."
— Israel Regardie *The Art of Magic*

The Tarot teaches about transformation through its symbols, dynamic archetypes of change, and the journey it portrays with its twists, turns, jumps and falls along life's path. I call this the "Sacred Journey of the Soul" which unfolds through the major arcana of the Tarot and radiates throughout the minor arcana.

Swiss psychoanalyst Carl C. Jung, mythologist Joseph Campbell, and other writers of the 20th Century revealed this path of transformation in their work, noting the "Hero's Journey" with its stages of development and change (see Chapter 3). Jung's writings on what he called our *Individuation* process, the personal "Alchemical" journey of one's soul, and the unfolding and discovery of one's authentic and deepest self, inspired Israel Regardie (Hermetic Order of the Golden Dawn, secretary to Aleister Crowley) to make the connection between magic, psychology and transformation of the individual.

In his little book, *The Art and Meaning of Magic*, Regardie lays out the four stages of magic, drawn from his extensive experience in the occult, then influenced by his study of Jung's stages of personal alchemy in therapeutic change.

Regardie's basic stages of magic:
  I.   *Divination − accessing intuition*
  II. *Evocation and Vision − evoking "spirits"*
  III. *Invocation − integrating the essence, union with God*
  IV. *Initiation − repeating the process with others*

This chapter will uncover these four states of magic and how they inform us about the potential in our journey through life then applies this wisdom to experience a Tarot reading more completely.

REGARDIE and the STAGES of MAGIC

Divination

"...Divination, the art of obtaining at a moment's notice any required type of information regarding the outcome of certain actions or events. Fortune telling so-called is an abuse. The sole purpose of the art is to develop the

intuitive faculties of the student to such an extent that
eventually all technical methods of divination may be
discarded."
— Israel Regardie *The Art of Magic*

According to Regardie, the objective of divination is the
development of the inner psychic faculty of intuition. When
we apply intuition, we build a bridge between our conscious
awareness and our higher self. We enhance our deeper
spiritual nature and our ability to tap our source of
inspiration and life, thus, making it available to our
ordinary awareness, to our conscious mind. As readers, we
use Tarot cards as a tool to tap into this initial stage of magic
and transformation.

"...divination is not ultimately concerned with mere
fortune-telling — nor even with divining the spiritual
causes in the background of material events..."
"Magic conceives of divinity as Spirit and Light and
Love."
— Israel Regardie *The Art of Magic*

Simply put, by developing our intuitive capacity, we
decrease the gap between the limitations of our human ego
and our divine nature, or God-like awareness. I think of
divination as communication with the Divine, whatever
Divine might mean to you, be it an outer deity, deep inner
nature, or more. *Webster's New Universal Unabridged
Dictionary* defines divinity as a study of religion, or
spirituality, as well as a quality or condition of being divine.
Reducing the power of divination to mere fortune-telling
deprives the reader and especially the client, of our most
precious gift, the depth of connection with love and light.
Without this light one is condemned to illusions and
attachments, much like XV The Devil, for fear of truly being
alive (notice that Devil spelled backwards is "Lived").

Evocation and Vision

> "The meaning of a myth resounds in its evoked
> associations, and if the scholar is to become aware of
> these, he must allow their counterparts to arise within
> himself from those regions of his nature he still shares
> with early man."
> — Joseph Campbell

The stage of *evocation* is more obscure and difficult than
divination. Spirits are evoked, stirred from their sleep, or
their roles are called into question. Once viewed, these
spirits can represent our greatest fears and nightmares, or
life's sweetest blessings.

Regardie relates these spirits with his study of Freud
and Jung and the term "complex," a constellation or group
of mental factors with a strong emotional charge, capable of
influencing conscious thought and behavior. In Jungian
psychology, this complex is called an *archetype*, a universal
pattern of experience. Each card in the Tarot deck is
associated with an archetypal law, lesson, or experience in
life.

This step in the magical way is to "personalize" the
spirits, to invest them with tangible shape and form, and to
give them a definite name and quality. In the reading, cards
are selected, characters are named, and identified with, or
disowned as other or evil.

> "...the purpose of Evocation is that some portion of the
> human psyche which has become deficient in a more or
> less important quality is made intentionally to stand out,
> as it were."
> — Israel Regardie *The Art of Magic*

Dynamic relationships emerge, with contrast and
duality becoming the tools of this stage. I call this the
"Dance of Duality." Once at least two distinct spirits are

evoked, they begin to dialogue or dance with each other, from their unique points of view. What is the meaning of them coming together? What awareness can they inspire in each other or merge together? How does one catalyze the other? Do they complete each other in some way?

These two spirits, characters, or cards represent a duality or split that invites healing, reconciliation, or merging. Duality comes in many forms, most notably: light and dark, day and night, good and bad, right and wrong, righteous and evil, this and that, me and you, us and them, feminine and masculine, inner and outer, life and death, etc. But duality is not always this simple. In a Tarot reading, it can appear as conscious and subconscious, familiar and unknown, easy and difficult, attraction and repulsion, victim and perpetrator, hero and villain, force and vulnerability, playful and serious, joy and sorrow, to name a few possibilities.

Jung saw this challenge of duality as a necessary step to psychic integration, and expressed that *consciousness itself is a product of the tension between opposites*. In other words, it is the contrast with other that gives rise to awareness, like a mirror, reflecting an image back to us so we have something to compare...the difference that makes a difference. When we consider this dynamic tension in a reading, we open the door to higher awareness and inner balance.

To illustrate this dynamic tension within a transformative Tarot reading here are a couple of examples:
1. Many Tarot layouts will have a card placement that represents what is "for" the querent, their ego identification with the issue. Another card placement will represent what is "against" the querent. The card that "crosses" the querent initiates this dynamic tension within the querent's identity.

2. The querent asks the cards to reveal something about an issue at their workplace. The cards that appear then take the querent in a different direction, perhaps looking at their relationship to their health. Now the querent's attention shifts from being the victim of a workplace drama to being responsible for the care of their own health. Are these two issues related? What will these issues reflect back to the querent about their choices in life?

Once this contrast of interests is established, the cards' spirits, or energies, begin to exchange, compare, even dance. What started as opposites begin to make inroads to understanding each other. How do these spirits or archetypes need each other? Are they dual aspects of the querent's inner life as well as their outer world? What kind of relationship might develop between the two? Is there hope for unification?

Thesis, Antithesis, and Synthesis

> "Regardless of subject matter, [Martin Luther] King never tired of moving from a one-sided thesis to a corrective, but also one-sided antithesis and finally to a more coherent synthesis beyond both."
> — L. Harold DeWolf *Bearing The Cross: Martin Luther King, Jr., and the Southern Christian Leadership Conference*

Hegel, the 19th century German philosopher, inspired by the logic of Classic Greek syllogism, developed the concept of the "dialectical method" which incorporates the process of "thesis, antithesis, and synthesis." A thesis can be seen as a single concept. This initial concept contains a form of incompleteness that gives rise to the antithesis as an opposing or conflicting element. A new concept, or a synthesis, arises from the contrast between the first two elements. It transcends the conflict by reconciling at a higher level the points of view contained in the thesis and antithesis. Hegel's method presents the idea that a conflict of opposites is a struggle between current and potential worlds.

Using the second example of the client's workplace issue above, the thesis might be "I need to keep my job, but I feel insecure about my position since the company is laying off people." The antithesis in the example showed up as a card requesting attention to the client's health. On the surface, the assumption might be that these two have nothing to do with each other, but once the dialogue between job and health develops a connection begins to emerge between the client's physical illness and their work. A new concept might arise from the client where they realize that the workplace is the source of their lack of wellbeing and they would rather move into a field that is more suited to their interests and creativity.

According to Rowena Pattee Kryder, in her book titled *Source - Visionary Interpretations of Global Creation Myths*, these basic themes appear as a sequence in major creation myths as "Creative Will," "Polarity" (conflict, sacrifice), and "Creation of Nature" (reconciliation), with an occasional forth stage, "Return to Source." Thesis, or *Divine Will*, appears as a dream, desire, vision, or the primary substance. Antithesis may be expressed as conflict, opposition, polarity, or a sacrifice. Synthesis then expresses the way invisible powers interact with one another as a reemergence, death and rebirth. To *Return to Source* is to transform, transcend, and return to God-head.

When a Tarot reader applies the awareness of dynamic tension to a reading, it becomes a dance, a story, personal myth, and ultimately a vision of possibility for the client's life at that moment. This vision was evoked by the dynamic interaction of the cards, symbols, spirits, and archetypes present in the reading.

> "The vision thus obtained corresponds generally to a sort of dream, experienced however in a fully conscious state."
> — Israel Regardie *The Art of Magic*

As in dreams, psychic difficulties or complexes are given some human, animal or other symbolic form. The art of magic and transformation is to dream while awake (Arnold Mindell, Ph.D.), raising our conscious awareness while having more access to personal choice and its inherent responsibility.

Carl Jung spent his lifetime studying dreams and the archetypal figures and stories that emerge in our dreamlife, individually and collectively. In the Tarot, each major arcana card represents an archetypal essence, such as trump III The Empress as the archetypal mother figure of the Tarot. Minor arcana cards can also evoke archetypal life energies, which may be expressed in daily activities and experiences. When Regardie describes the complexes as spirits, what psychology calls archetypes, he speaks of the power in these spirits to influence our conscious thoughts and behaviors. Jung and other psychological professionals would add that our subconscious impulses are equally influenced by these archetypal energies. Thus, the Tarot is a magical tool to bring these energies to the surface for our conscious awareness to explore.

Each time a card is turned over in a Tarot reading, the card has the potential of evoking a response. If you are reading for yourself, pay attention to your feelings, notice your reaction, an association that emerges, or a memory that may be triggered by the symbols in the card. At that moment, the card is evoking an experience within you.

If reading for another, the same possibilities for evoking spirits, or energy, are present. Figures from the client's dreaming are coming to the surface to be named and related. There is a resonance, be it positive, negative, or neutral, with the message the card represents. This is a deeply intuitive procedure that does not rely on card knowledge. In fact, it is best to forget for the moment anything you may already know about the intended meaning of the card. As the reader, I suggest you keep your thoughts on the "back burner" to allow your client to explore their first impression.

You are invited to notice that the energy and associations come from the client, not the card. The card is merely a catalyst for this response, thus it does not matter whether the designated interpretation of the card is based on Tarot knowledge. An excellent resource for experimenting with some of these techniques for drawing intuitive information from a card is Mary Greer's book, *21 Ways to Read a Tarot Card*. In this unique offering, she explores methods for focusing on the symbols, emotions, metaphors, and meanings that may arise for the client with their cards.

An important guideline for the reader to keep in mind, that will support the client's experience of the card, is to allow the space and time necessary for the client to personalize the spirit of the card, developing a subjective experience with its essence. In order for this to be successful, I suggest the reader withhold any response to the card and take a back seat to the client's relationship with that card. In this sequence, the client comes first, while the reader follows the client's cues. Whose reading is it? Whose spirit is being called in this magical process?

Once several spirits have been evoked, either through a one-card reading, or through the process of laying cards in a spread, the spirits begin to interact with each other.

Dynamic qualities from each archetype emerge and contrast or blend with the other energies in the card or cards, laying the groundwork for a new pathway as the story unfolds.

Examples of How Spirits "Dance" in a Reading:

Two-card reading

A woman selects III The Empress and the Ace of Pentacles. She associates The Empress with nurturing the Earth, while the Ace of Pentacles represents a new project. She contemplates how these two wish to work together. Using the mode of dynamic tension and developing a new synthesis, these contrasting archetypes begin to communicate and create a bridge of understanding within her. The idea of creating a new garden materializes, satisfying her need to honor the Earth while investing creative energy in a productive endeavor.

One-card self-reading

A man shuffles the Tarot cards and thinks about his question. He asks for guidance on making a commitment to a group. One consideration is the time involvement required, while the other is a shared value he has with the group. He turns over the Three of Swords card and focuses on the swords: two point down, forming an "X" as they cross the center of the card, while the third points up through the center of the card and divides it in two. At first, he associates the "X" with a message that says, "sign your name by the X," a reflection of the commitment side of his query. Emotionally, he might feel hesitant and a little apprehensive. It seems like a permanent or irrevocable contract. Now he ponders the third sword, which pierces the other two up through the center. This inspires him to follow the feeling of commitment, but to follow his own path, not to feel split between commitment to the group or not. He now associates the "X" with the idea of truth and commitment to his values. Feelings of pride and conviction overtake the hesitancy of his first impression. He merges the feeling of commitment from the first impression with the freedom of finding his own path. Rather than joining the group, he finds a new way to express his conviction and feels balance with his choice.

Invocation

> "The inevitable end of Magic is identical in the conceived of in Mysticism, union with God-head."
> — Israel Regardie *The Art of Magic*

Invocation is our homecoming, returning to a holistic awareness of self and spirit, a "Return to Source," as expressed by Kryder. Regardie explains, invocation has "…as its objective the necessary assimilation of the unconscious content of the psyche into normal consciousness. Its object, also, is the enlarging of the horizon of the mind by enlarging the student's intellectual conceptions of the nature of the universe."

To *invoke* the vision evoked by the second stage "dance" of the magical art is a process of integration and inner identification with all parts of the dreaming, the awoken spirits. No longer do we fall into dualistic preferences for one or the other, but find a middle way that includes the essence of both and recognizes them as once partially or completely hidden aspects of oneself. Then, "as above, so below," we identify our oneness with the Divine.

In Jungian psychology, this journey is called the individuation process. Here we reclaim our "shadow," or disowned parts of our psyche in order to be more whole. When we are able to integrate the various and challenging aspects of our lives, they no longer have power over us. We move away from dualistic thinking and reacting, while drawing closer to the divinity of "Spirit and Light and Love." Tarot as a magical tool inspires such awareness.

Various techniques may be employed to reach integration. Meditation upon an image that symbolizes your newfound identity may provide an outer mirror to inspire inner awareness. Re-membering the vision or story of your magical course and imaging the actualization of this new pathway in life can be the first step to walking it in your outer life. Some people find great support in joining groups of like-spirited folks who empower a new way of being.

Now that the spirits of the Tarot cards have been evoked and danced, we are asked to integrate their guidance and wisdom into life. If the client has divined their own meaning of the cards, conceived of unique solutions, and taken personal responsibility for their decisions, then they are on the road to integrating the guidance of the spirits in their reading. This emphasizes the importance of the reader taking a more passive yet supportive role in the reading process. A professional Tarot reader can be like a Sacred Doula, or midwife, for the client's experience.

As with classical counseling, it is important that clients discover their own solutions. It is ineffective to feed them solutions, for that only involves the head, not the heart. Once a client invests personal feelings and vision with the issues being explored, the result is more personal and empowering. Here is the magic that Regardie teaches. We each have the capacity to deeply explore the spirits at work in our psyches and to resolve our personal challenges in a way that honors life's process, thus bringing us closer to our divine selves, or what Regardie calls "God-head."

The individuation process is completed with this third stage applying the art of magic and transformation. We unite process and outcome, journey and destination, wave and particle of quantum physics, the alpha and the omega, the individual with the Divine, as we realize wholeness and holiness.

> "If the essence and perfection of all good are comprehended in the gods, and the first and ancient power of them is with us priests (i.e. magicians) and if by those who similarly adhere to more excellent natures and genuinely obtain a union with them, the beginning and end of all good is earnestly pursued; if this be the case, here the contemplation of truth, and the possession of intellectual science are to be found. And a knowledge of the Gods is accompanied with . . . the knowledge of ourselves."
> — Iamblichus

Initiation

Once we travel this path of magic, identify the parts and bringing them into harmony and integration, we then develop the strength, insight and patience to assist others in their "Sacred Journey." The student becomes the teacher, the Tarot client becomes the reader, *and* we guide the process for others by becoming a mentor for their learning. Experience is the best teacher and as teachers we then support the opportunity for others to brave their shadows, evoke their unconscious spirits, and guide them to new experiences and fuller awareness.

To get you started on this magical journey, in this next session I would like to introduce you to these stages of transformation as they may appear in a reading. Chapter 6 offers greater detail on Regardie's method applied in sample sessions.

The FOUR STAGES of MAGIC in a READING

Much like the energy of trump I Magician and the Aces of each suit of the Tarot, if we are open to this gift, there is potential for magic and transformation in every Tarot reading.

I'd like to relate the four stages of magic to the process of reading and invite you to consider their application. There are as many variations on this process as there are people or readings. But the following examples may give you a taste of how magical processes may materialize. If you are interested in experiencing this method of reading Tarot or receiving personal instruction on the finer details of this work, please contact me through my website: TarotCounseling.org

Divination — Choosing to have a reading is this first step for the querent, opening the door to the potential for change in their life, and approaching the unknown. Naming the issue deepens that divine opening by identifying what part of their life pattern has the spotlight shining upon it. Much like a muscle that finally exclaims, "Ouch, I've had enough, stop straining me," the querent's attention is drawn to the sore spot in their life.

Not every reading begins with a challenge or issues. If the querent is proactive and looking for guidance in the Tarot through reading the cards, what is instigated is the next step of their process of awareness. And, thus, the veil begins to dissolve…

Evocation — Identifying the issue or the focus of the reading, as well as selecting cards to represent the energies at work in this drama, evokes feelings, associations, or characters from the querent's life. The spirits in the background are now brought to the surface and made more apparent. This is the stage of conscious awareness as the querent dances with the archetypes.

We can't address what we do not acknowledge. As John Gray Ph.D. says, "What you feel, you can heal." What we hide, we are doomed to repeat. By ignoring the triggers for our unconscious reactions, we risk developing cycling patterns of self-medicating thoughts and behaviors. We comfort, or self-medicate, with people, places and things that distract us from the source of our disturbance. For example, a person feels lonely and goes to the local pub for a brew. Whether it is the beer or the people occupying the pub, they fill their inner void with a substitute to distract them from feeling the distress of loneliness.

Tarot cards, when used as a tool to raise awareness and capture little glimpses of distress for the querent, can be a gentle beginning on the journey of self-discovery and wholeness. But, as with any double-edged sword, Tarot cards can cut the other way, falling into the category of self-medication and obsession by *relying* on the cards to direct the querent's life. In this case, the reading, or the reader, may become the object of desire, a substitute for personal fulfillment, the opposite of wholeness.

Once the archetypes, spirits, or the client's feelings are evoked by the cards drawn, a dance begins to develop between the cards, client, and reader. Meaning and magic are woven together. The reader guides the client into connecting with each card as they reflect upon the initial issue. The client makes personal associations with each card and its placement in the spread to uncover what part of the path the client is currently exploring. A story emerges.

Will the client choose to see new possibilities or return to the comfort of the known? The response comes in the next stage, Invocation, where the brave of heart and open minded delve.

Invocation — The wisdom in the cards has been revealed. The querent received the message, but how does the querent begin to unite with this new possibility? To invoke the power of the reading, the querent finds personal meaning and begins the stage of integration. The reader can assist the client to ground this awareness by asking where they might apply this new information, or how this new perception wishes to come through in life. Applying the message of the reading to a real life situation will engage the querent in imagining new possibilities, away from the old known cycle of behavior in their life, to begin breaking old comfortable chains. A new perspective can emerge which empowers the querent to establish a more authentic self-image and direction.

Initiation — Now that the querent has experienced this magical journey, faced fears, and envisioned new pathways, the process becomes less strange and actually more empowering, which invites a return to the focus of discovering the querent's authentic self.

This part of the journey is where the reading transcends the cards completely, when their essence is carried within the querent as the living embodiment of their wisdom. Transformation has been achieved. Who arrived and was initiated into this experience is not the same person as who walks away holding the cards in their heart and mind's eye.

Being touched by the cards, a client might decide to take up Tarot as a tool to support the continuation of their journey through life. And as such, the client becomes the channel for Divine wisdom to work its magic and possibly to touch others.

Now that we know that magic is afoot, we are ready to move forward, to jump into the alchemical pot of transformation and change, to go beyond any previous conception of who we are or what life is about…much like the lessons of life as told through "Sacred Journey of Your Soul" of the Tarot's major arcana.

> "The end result is illumination and ecstasy, a transporting of the consciousness of the Magus to an identity with the consciousness of all that lives, an ineffable union with the Light, the One Life that permeates all space and time."
> — Israel Regardie *Magic in East and West*

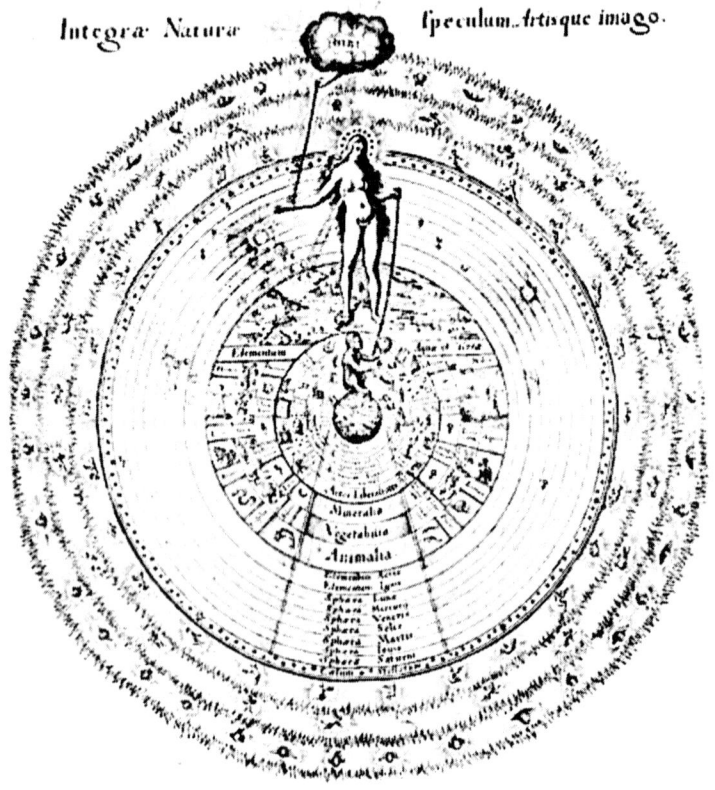

3

Jung and Alchemy

"To confront a person with his own shadow is to show him his own light."
— Carl G. Jung "Good and Evil in Analytical Psychology" CW 10. *Civilization in Transition*

Swiss psychoanalyst Carl G. Jung has had a profound influence on modern psychology, but his reach transcends this field. Jung's exploration of the magic in Tarot has had a significant impact on the way many Tarot readers perceive the meaning, or to use his concept—archetypal awareness—of each card.

For the Introduction to Sallie Nichols preeminent work, *Jung and Tarot – An Archetypal Journey*, Laurens van der Post wrote, "He [Jung] recognized at once, as he did in so many other games and primordial attempts at divination of the unseen and the future, that Tarot had its origin and anticipation in profound patterns of the collective unconscious with access to potentials of increased awareness uniquely at the disposal of these patterns. It was another of those non-rational bridges across the apparent divide between conscious and unconscious to carry night and day what should be the growing stream of traffic between darkness and light."

Through Jung's study and writing on alchemy, active imagination, dreams, individuation, symbolism, synchronicity, and the journey of transformation, many mental health professionals and Tarot counselors alike have developed tools to better support the life journey of their clients.

Jung, Individuation, and the Shadow

Jung described the transformative art of alchemy in psychotherapeutic terms by drawing an analogy to what he called the *individuation* process.

Individuation is "…the process by which a person becomes an in-dividual, that is, a separate indivisible unity or whole." (Carl C. Jung) Clients apply the tools of free association, active imagination, dreamwork, or in our case, Tarot cards, to transform the personal and collective unconscious to a greater awareness of Self. Individuation, as a soulful process, promotes holistic healing which can support integration of the psyche.

Feeling whole, embracing one's totality, including the less attractive or shy parts of oneself, is a powerful underlying message of Tarot as a visual book of wisdom. It informs the student of Tarot not only how to uncover their personal potential, but also to bring this awareness to readings with others.

Most Tarot readings consist of reportage and insight by the reader, but then miss the golden opportunity to support a deeply personal experience for the client that helps to transform their relationship to the original issue. In addition, the information and results of the reading tend to be delivered in dualistic terms of good or bad, right or wrong, thus reducing the wealth of the Tarot's wisdom to simplistic and superficial conclusions.

Transformative Tarot Counseling (TTC) encourages us to move *through* our "shadow" material to find a personal experience in the cards that brings us closer to our light. In order to have this deeper knowing of Tarot wisdom, it requires expanding our awareness to include all resources that may enhance card wisdom, to continually question our assumptions, and to reinforce our willingness to go into the unknown.

> "A man who is unconscious of himself acts in a blind, instinctive way and is in addition fooled by all the illusions that arise when he sees everything that he is not conscious of in himself coming to meet him from outside as projections upon his neighbour."
> — Carl G. Jung "The Philosophical Tree" CW 13: *Alchemical Studies*

What is the **shadow**? It is that part of our personality we cannot bare to see for it is in violation of the idealized Self. As an unconscious personality, shadow material contains repressed energy, often depressed emotions, which can hold the key to our hidden powers. Not being integrated or even acknowledged by the conscious mind, the shadow resides in the unconscious, occasionally acting out or projecting onto others those unknown parts. Maryanne Williams teaches, "Our deepest fear is not that we are inadequate. Our deepest fear is that we are powerful beyond measure."

For example, someone does not like their manager where they work because their ideas are never heard. But, in this example, the shadow is their resistance to identifying with being an authority and finding an occupation that reflects this aspect of their potential.

Alchemy

"Alchemy is the art of transmutating base metals into silver or gold by freeing the 'impurities."
—Johannes Fabricius *Alchemy - The Medieval Alchemists and their Royal Art*

Alchemy, the ancient science for creating gold from base metals, is simultaneously an esoteric tradition that offers metaphor and meaning to transformational styles of working with people and change. By understanding the ancient wisdom symbolized in the alchemical process and the steps involved in completing the journey of change it represents, we find a pattern for exploring personal challenges and draw strength in knowing there may be meaning in the madness of chaos and change in life, for which we ultimately must find our own deep truth.

Like the shadow, impurities are the parts of our psyches that we have not integrated, our unloved aspects that need to be transformed. Alchemy is a powerful metaphor for the process of soul retrieval and self-love.

"To reach the knowledge of the Creator is to part the veil and transmute the obscurity of ignorance into the light of wisdom. To attain that supreme wisdom is consciously to become one with God in love; to live to love."
— Stanislas Klossowski de Rola *Alchemy - The Secret Art*

Jung introduced us to the symbolic quest for individuation in alchemy. To Jung, this alchemical journey is focused on becoming aware of ourselves as individuals, being able to act on our psychic uniqueness, and to reach a state of wholeness. He correlated the stages of the alchemical procedure with the steps to human integration of conscious with unconscious material (shadow), and moving beyond our ego identity to reach the Self's higher potential.

"The alchemists in their search for gold discovered many other things of greater value."
— Arthur Schopenhauer

Alchemists were the original chemists and philosophers. To the outer world they were involved with the practice of science as they experimented with mercury and other materials with the objective of turning these base metals into gold. On the metaphysical level, the object of their study was to discover the golden elixir of eternal life. In this way, Jung was a modern alchemist who mixed, distilled, and purified our understanding of our greatest potential, the golden light of our being.

Alchemy and the Stages of Transformation

To study alchemy is to study the art of transformation. In order to reveal the possible depth of working with the Tarot, a greater understanding of the basic alchemical stages is essential. Every stage of alchemy correlates to a part in the sequence of a transformative reading, with each step building upon the previous one.

The process of alchemy begins with the *Nigredo,* the blackening, where the *prima materia* is placed in a pot or cauldron and heated. Jung likened this material to the unconscious, containing the *massa confusa,* or chaos, without order. Shadow material emerges as the archetypes at work are revealed. It is a time of initiation and self-reflection where materialistic ego may begin to dissolve.

The Nigredo stage is associated with the querent's presenting problem, or what the querent is seeking help to change. In Tarot counseling, we can think of this stage as the query or question the client is asking, the issue that is placed on the table. It represents the unknown and unformed state of the client and their story. The Tarot cards are laid down with the reading in an open state without interpretation. Magic is afoot!

The next stage is the *Albedo*, the whitening, or reflected light, personified by the "white lunar queen." In alchemy, this is where the pot has been heated. Melting and blending combines the base materials, purifying the black material to a white appearance. At this point, the alchemist may choose to repeat the process to purify it further.

When counseling the Tarot client, the conscious or traditional understanding of each card and its position in the layout lends insight when shared with the client. I believe this is the most basic and least personal level of Tarot reading. The cards are interpreted *for* the client, bringing the knowledge of the cards to light. But, it often does not include the client's perceptions or feelings. Therefore this stage only offers insight without support for integration. The information is recognized, but not personalized. There is no actual change in the client and the effect of the reading may fade soon after the client walks away.

I would like to take a moment to distinguish two styles of reading the Tarot mentioned previously in this publication. Insight-oriented Tarot reading is interpretive and tells the client what the cards mean. This type of reading stops at the Albedo stage of the alchemical process. In contrast, TTC offers an *experience* of the cards' message, the evoked spirits, and their *dance*. It supports the transformative potential of the client (and the reader). Further distinction can be made by imagining the typical Tarot reading as satisfying the mind, from the neck up, while TTC is a full-body experience including the body, mind, heart, and spirit, a more integrative prospect.

The next alchemical stage is the *Rubedo*, the "red king" or reddening, which occurred when the alchemist allowed the materials to cook to a red-hot state. That metaphorically represents the beginning of integrating new knowledge. The materials were heated to such a degree that they blended and purified into a new form, with no resemblance to their original form. In the previous chapter on magic and change, that process was explained as the dynamic tension and subsequent synthesis of the evoked spirits.

In working with the Tarot, new understanding comes when the querent is personally involved in the reading. This is accomplished in a variety of ways: drawing out the client by asking for personal associations to the cards, using active imagination, active listening and then by artfully weaving this personal material into the story of the reading. By supporting any emotion that naturally arises and including both the client's and the reader's intuitive impressions in the mixture a deeper story unfolds. The *experience* of the reading becomes more significant than the interpretation of the Tarot cards. Now, the spirits spin and blend together.

The *Great Conjunctio* (sometimes considered a stage) of alchemy represents our journey's final goal, the gold in the alchemical motif. Symbolically, this stage culminates with the marriage (union/synthesis) of the *white lunar queen* (insight/inner light of trump XVIII The Moon) and the *red king* (enlightenment/stabilized awareness of trump XIX The Sun) culminating with the hermaphroditic *Stone of the Philosophers* (individuation/homecoming of trump XXI The World). This final product is what the alchemists called the Philosopher's Stone, the gold of enlightenment. Psychologically, this heralds the completion of the individuation process when we have discovered our true Self internally and begin to live this truth externally in the world. We walk through life with greater awareness, congruence and authenticity.

For the Tarot querent, the Philosopher's Stone is represented by the capacity to invoke the archetypes from the reading and allow this experience to change their life. The knowledge of the cards and the wisdom of personal experience are integrated, personalized, and acted upon in the querent's internal and external life. The gold is the querent's capacity to shine their light in the world from within and transform the original issue into a creative opportunity, becoming the master of one's Self.

While alchemy offers a valuable metaphor for tracing the transformative journey inherent in life, it takes practice and skill development to apply this model to Tarot work. Chapter 6 provides sample TTC readings to illustrate the alchemical stages. In the following chapter we will explore the counseling skills that support this transformative potential.

4

Counseling Skills and Awareness

"I have often been very moved by how you can help people *to help themselves* by helping them to discover their own truth, a truth whose richness, sweetness, and profundity they may never have suspected."
— Sogyal Rimpoche *The Tibetan Book of Living and Dying*

Tarot reading and the ethics involved are a huge and often controversial topic. Whether we choose to think about it or not, we should keep ethical considerations in mind when we offer readings to others. The broad subject of ethics includes principles, morals, beliefs, and values, which this chapter addresses in context of counseling skills as practiced within Tarot (or other consulting) sessions.

My perspective and experience is informed by 40 years of Tarot study combined with 24 years of training and practice in psychotherapy, hypnotherapy, dreamwork, and counseling. This chapter focuses on Tarot "Counseling Skills", while the next chapter will discuss ethical guidelines, codes and legal considerations of Tarot readings.

Why would a Tarot reader be concerned with such concepts? Technically, the moment the reader offers their service to the general public, they are working with clients who are most likely seeking *advice*. Unless both the reader and client are informed and consent to the session as purely entertainment, it may begin to slip into questionable ethics or legal territory. For this reason, I recommend professional readers acquaint themselves with counseling skills and related ethical guidelines.

Tarot Counseling or Predictive Reading

The diversity of reading styles in modern Tarot work run the gamut between these two modalities, from counseling-type skills to prediction-oriented readings. Each style has its pros and cons for readers and clients.

In a typical reading, the client brings a question that represents an issue with money, health, relationships, decision-making, etc. The reader follows the ritual of card selection and display, and then proceeds to directly answer the client's question, based on card knowledge, intuitive skills, or psychic guidance. The reader's focus is on the interpretation of the cards and their message being "right" or "accurate" while avoiding being "wrong," especially when utilizing predictions.

In contrast, a counseling-based approach to working with the client incorporates skills of guidance, supporting the client's ability to work through issues and helps them see life from a different perspective with the assistance and inspiration of the cards. Tarot readers with counseling skills know, in essence, they are assisting the journey of the client's soul, while tending to the psyche. Overall, there is a greater sense of *following* the client, listening to their impressions, honoring subtle feelings, and empowering the client's interpretation of the meaning in their reading. No predictions or prescriptions are made.

Is there a time when it is appropriate to introduce psychic information or state a direction with your clients in a counseling-based approach? Yes, but with great awareness and reserve. For instance, if in a reading your client reaches an impasse while you have a psychic message you believe needs to be delivered, you may introduce the new information by asking the client for permission to share. If permission is granted, you might say something like, "I'm not sure if this is right for you, but I have a strong sense that..." In this way you have presented the new information from a clearly subjective perspective and involved the client's power of permission to include this information in the reading. There are other examples, such as when a reader makes a strong directive for the purpose of challenging the client's point of view. This is best delivered by a skilled counselor who understands the technique of being a catalyst for change with the ethics and follow-through to support the client's subsequent reaction.

Following or Leading the Client in a Reading

The practice of "following" a client is a new concept for many Tarot readers, while it is a cornerstone of traditional counseling modalities. If counseling were simply a matter of giving clients the "right" answer, life would be so much easier.

In reality, people do not usually adopt "answers," and tend to cycle within their patterns of behavior and life choices. Frequently returning clients often present the same issues, and thus sustain a Tarot reader's business. If the reader gave "good" advice, then why does the client keep having the same questions and problems? It is like putting a band-aid on a sore, when the client keeps peeling it off. Real healing never actually takes place.

As described in Chapter 1, a counselor's job is not to merely give simple advice or direct clients on what to do. They assist clients to engage in their own process of uncovering issues and support them to find their personal power.

"Leading" is the process of giving information without the emotional or intellectual engagement of the client. It feeds the curiosity of the client, from the head up, but does not necessarily impact the whole being. Leading happens when the reader interprets the cards *for* the client, gives advice, makes directives, reveals predictions, or just stays within the knowledge base of the reader. I call this a reader-centered, one-way communication, for it comes *from* the reader *to* the client with less emphasis on developing a dynamic relationship or feedback loop.

In contrast, "following" the client in a Tarot reading utilizes deep listening skills, which invites the client to interact with the cards from their unique perspective, and stretches the reader's imagination to incorporate information from both the client and the cards. The patience of listening is a more challenging approach for the reader who may be accustomed to acting as the authority in a reading. But please keep in mind that this client-centered approach involves the client in the reading process, engages them in their own intuitive relationship with the cards, and then supports their own discovery of solutions, actions, or meaning in a more powerful way. In this process of following, the reader takes a back seat to the client and the cards, while allowing the client's inner wisdom to shine forth with support from the reader's experienced guidance. This also means that the client works more in their reading, and is not the passive recipient. This removes the tendency for the client to become dependent upon the reader.

How I Engage the Client in their Reading

During a reading, the cards are turned over and gazed upon one at a time. As the card is turned, I ask the client to notice her, or his, first impression of the card, such as a thought, feeling, reaction, or association. This invites the client to tune into their intuitive awareness without putting them on the spot by requesting a "meaning" or interpretation. The client easily engages in their own reading which gets their intuitive and emotional juices flowing.

As the reader, I have knowledge of a diversity of associations and meanings for each card. With the client's first impression in mind, I can select information about that card which will be most useful for that client. This honors the diversity of perspectives and needs for each client. As we continue to interact, I further layer intuitive information or insights that come to me. I find it really is not a one-size-fits-all approach. It is a co-creative process, rather than a one-way street where the reader has all the answers. With this approach, the client can more readily accept responsibility for their experience, their personal interpretation, and the resulting choice they make with the confidence of knowing their answer is their own.

How might this look in a reading? Following is a brief example of how I might engage a client in a reading:

A client comes for a reading to explore guidance on the topic of a career choice. I turn a card over for my client, and the first thing she notices is "balloons." (By the way, it doesn't matter if there are actually balloons in the card). I then ask the client to say more about the balloons, and she begins to talk about freedom and feeling lighter. One career choice for which the client sought guidance was creating her own business. The client expresses feeling light and happy while discussing that possibility, compared to other options, which seem to inspire a heavier sensation. Next we look at the card selected, trump I Magician. I describe the Magician's ability to make things manifest when one focuses all her "magic wand" energy on one goal. My statement reflects support for the client's personal confidence in making her own choice to start a business. The client's decision was already made by her own awareness of what felt "right," and not based upon me making a prediction or telling her what to do. Because the reading was grounded in her body experience, stimulated by the reading, she has a better chance of remembering and accessing that experience with confidence, then following the guidance of her experience for further decisions on the topic.

Chapter 6 offers sample readings to illustrate a variety of ways to support clients with client-centered techniques.

COUNSELING SKILLS for READERS

Many counseling skills are very applicable to working with Tarot clients. For example, the care and sensitivity involved in interacting with someone's psyche is a consideration that both professional counselors and Tarot readers have in common. When a client is asking for *advice*, especially on vulnerable topics such as relationships or life direction choices with life-long consequences, the reader is definitely treading on touchy ground and needs to be aware and sensitive to the client. Regardless of one's preferred Tarot reading style, all readers can benefit from the exploration of the classic counseling techniques described below.

Traditional Counseling Skills

Listening — Effectively listening to another is to be attentive and observant with a compassionate presence. This cannot be accomplished if the reader is focused on their own words, thoughts, strategies, etc. For a reader who does not identify with being particularly psychic, listening deeply inside one's self is a powerful channel for receiving intuitive information. Listening skills also help us pay attention to the client's level of presence or engagement, which will help detect unspoken boundaries. Boundaries are addressed in Chapter 5 on counseling ethics.

Patience — Listening requires patience for the reader, as well as the client. At the beginning of a reading, agree to a predetermined amount of time for the reading. Doing so helps create a safe container for working together. Make sure the time is designed to provide sufficient space for patience, stillness, and listening deeply. This will allow both reader and client enough time to go into the subject of the reading and the card details in such a way that the experience is complete, yet not so long that it becomes overwhelming.

Blank Access — In counseling, a technique called "Blank Access" is often used. It is the art of being purposefully vague and free of content, in order to inspire the client to fill in the blank and find their own answer. It requires a degree of vagueness from the reader to support the client to find meaning or personal truth. Sometimes it sounds like "Umm," or "Interesting," or "Can you say more?"

Awareness — Many readers are excellent at being aware of their intuitive knowing or psychic impressions. As a counseling skill, awareness means to be truly awake and present in the midst of a reading. This allows the reader to notice subtle communications as well as the client's intended and unintended communication. E.g., when a card is revealed and the client's eyes begin to tear-up a little. You can then pause and reflect back to the client noticing there may be some feelings involved with the card. If there is an opening or receptivity by the client, continue to find out more about the client's feelings, and connect that to card knowledge. Be patient and respect any boundary the client may have, whether asserted or implied. Boundaries will be further addressed in the next chapter.

Descriptive, not prescriptive — To be purely descriptive is a challenging skill for it requires the reader to withhold judgments, i.e., prejudices, predetermined opinions, and dualistic leanings (more on duality at the end of this chapter). This also includes assumptions about card meaning. In a prescriptive style reading, the client might select the Three of Swords card (Waite-Smith), and the reader immediately reports an interpretation about "Sorrow." Instead, a descriptive variant involves examining the card as if for the first time and naming the "bare bones" details. Here, the reader would note that there is a red heart in the center of the card with three metal swords piercing the heart, from the top down and from the left, center, and right, intersecting behind it, with three or more clouds at the top of the card with rain falling from them, etc. To combine observation with description in this example would include noticing that the client smiled when the card was turned and had a positive association to the image.

Transference and Counter-transference — This concept is a classic tool and occasional concern for professional counselors. Briefly, transference occurs when the client projects a role onto the counselor, such as filling a mother role. Counter-transference occurs when the counselor in return projects a role onto the client, such as a child or younger sibling. In a Tarot reading we might look at this process in terms of attraction, roles, power dynamics, and dependency. One such aspect is the reader's ability to differentiate what is the client's material and what is the reader's. For example, during the reading you notice that you begin to feel anxious, although before working with the client you were calm. Perhaps you are subconsciously feeling the client's emotional state. If you know yourself well enough to perceive that it is not *your* anxiety, then you have more awareness and choices for interacting with the client's mood or issue.

Serving the client or self-serving — This is what I differentiate as client-centered styles or reader-centered styles, respectfully. If the reader objectively examines the level of ego attachment involved with their work, especially in terms of being "right" or accurate in their prediction or projection, they may find a degree of self-service in the thrill or validation of being right, as well as in the drama of being wrong. Serving the client is accomplished by the reader *following* instead of leading the client. My focus when working with a client is "How can I best support you?"

"Metaskills" and Their Importance in Readings

Process Work, formerly Process-oriented Psychology, developed by Dr. Arnold Mindell, is a modality of psychotherapy I have studied and practiced since 1988. Dr. Amy Mindell, Arny's wife and teaching partner, has expanded this body of theory with her important book *Metaskills: The Spiritual Art of Therapy.*

Metaskills is a term coined by Amy, referring to conscious "feeling-oriented" attitudes counselors may access during their work. These skills require courage and commitment to excellence. Some skills may come naturally, while others need more practice. Metaskills are the most powerful tools the reader can apply to their Tarot work, and are also really helpful life skills. The following concepts are metaskills with examples of how they can support Tarot professionals in readings.

Compassion — is when the reader cares for and attends to all aspects of the reading and client. This includes aspects that may be considered difficult or unpleasant, sometimes called the "Shadow" (a term explored in Chapters 2 & 3). Part of this skill is the reader's willingness to be more aware of the client and their reading, in a non-judgmental way. Example, the client sits down for a reading with you and is wearing a t-shirt with a political slogan that represents a point of view that is opposite of your own. If it disturbs your feelings, you may find it difficult to focus fully on the reading. What if you allow your awareness to expand by compassionately considering the t-shirt slogan as one more symbol to blend into the reading? It then becomes a source of information instead of obstructing your awareness in the reading.

Beginner's Mind — refers to the Zen attitude of an open and unbiased mind and heart. It is not limited by knowledge. In it, the reader sees life fresh and with new eyes, aware of many possibilities. Mary Greer's book, *21 Ways to Read a Tarot Card,* is a great illustration for beginner's mind, because it offers a multitude of ways to work with cards from different perspectives.

Play — refers to a sense of freedom, spontaneity, and ability to be light-hearted. Playing with cards is natural for many folks and helps us not take the process too seriously. James Wanless, Ph.D., "Captain Pick a Card" (*Voyager Tarot*), is a prime model of a playful approach to working with Tarot and clients.

Humor — is helpful for making life playful and funny; the reader plays the fool or abandons the rules. We might say this is trump 0 The Fool's way of reading the cards. Injecting a little humor into the reading style allows it to be fun, nonsensical, without an authoritative attitude.

Detachment — permits the reader to release from the situation, allowing observation without judgment. Too often the reader focuses on the client's presenting question or story. In some cases, this is where boundaries get blurred, because the reader becomes emotionally involved with the client's story. It could be more helpful to release from the content or drama in order to see a new perspective that spontaneously wishes to emerge. Developing the skills of observation with compassion naturally leads to detachment in the reading relationship.

Creativity — A free mind is a creative mind. When the reader removes judgment, prejudice, assumptions and knowledge, what remains is an open, creative space where new possibilities have an opportunity to arise. The cards and client become co-creators in the process of the reading.

Fluidity & Stillness — "The fluid therapist has a still center that perceives the emergence of new information. She remains awake in the midst of change." – Amy Mindell, Ph.D. Such fluidity may be likened to the element of water, as viewed symbolically in the Tarot. Tarot professionals can benefit from developing a more flowing and fluid style of merging the client's input and shared intuitions, with knowledge of the cards.

Balance — Much like with the lessons in trump VIII Balance or Adjustment (also XI Justice), balance entails the reader's awareness of equal, yet contrasting aspects of an issue or perspective. The reader utilizes this skill to access a middle way, usually between dualistic options. The reader also needs to find balance between inner awareness and the outer world, the reading and the client, action and stillness, technique and spirituality.

This has been a brief introduction to many of the counseling skills from which the Tarot professional and their clients could benefit, if integrated into their reading style. I encourage you to experiment and discover which techniques best suit your interests. To complete the professional reading, counseling ethics are an important consideration. Chapter 5 introduces various aspects of ethics as they apply to the reader and the responsibilities involved with conducting their service.

5

Ethics and Responsibilities for Readers

"Avoid those pretenders who decide for you; take the reins in your own hands. You have to decide. In fact, in that very decisiveness, your soul is born. When others decide for you, your soul remains asleep and dull. When you start deciding on your own, a sharpness arises."
— Osho

In Chapter 4 we explored counseling skills and their relationship to Tarot reading. With these tools under our belt, let's now look at ethical considerations for Tarot practitioners who engage in professional readings from a counseling point of view.

Tarot reading ethics is a topic I feel strongly about and promote for all metaphysical consultants. Personally, I'm not in favor of standardized rules for practicing ethics, for I know there is a diversity of readers and reading styles in the world meeting a variety of needs, but the responsibility to honor the needs and boundaries of the client is paramount. In the case of practicing Tarot readings in the public domain, ignorance of legal rules is not a valid defense, a topic that will be addressed at the end of this chapter.

The first year of my graduate studies (Master of Arts in Counseling Psychology) required a "Professional Ethics in Counseling" course. Students examined several models of ethical considerations, from moral and social motivations, to the "Pillars of Responsibility," along with legal and licensure requirements for counseling professionals. Through continuing my educational training, I have expanded my understanding and use of ethics. This includes my work with Tarot clients, to whom I extend the same respect and responsible service.

In this chapter I divide the subject of reading ethics into four main areas; ethical guidelines, power dynamics, boundaries, and legal issues.

ETHICAL GUIDELINES

Whether you choose to think about it or not, there are ever present ethical considerations when offering readings to others. Ethics is defined as a personal or group philosophy reflecting values relating to human conduct and interactions. It includes motives as well as actions. Organizations, such as the American Tarot Association (ATA) and many individual Tarot sites list a "Code of Ethics" that cover variations on "do no harm," honesty, confidentiality, and scope of practice. Often they vary from one reader to another, but these guidelines deserve review and consideration.

General areas considered in the Tarot reader's ethical standards:
- Personal philosophy, values and belief system.
- Philosophy and values about the cards or their use.

- Areas of expertise, special skills, professional background, and training.
- Personal style and approach to working with the cards.
- Personal style and approach to working with clients.
- Rights and responsibilities of the reader.
- Rights and responsibilities of clients.
- Payment arrangement or exchange of energy.
- Legal parameters.

The following are two examples from the ATA Code of Ethics:

1. "I will recommend clients consult a licensed professional for advice of a legal, financial, medical, or psychological nature that I am not qualified to provide. If trained in one of these areas, I will clearly differentiate between the tarot reading and any professional advice additionally provided."

2. "I will keep confidential the names of clients and all information shared or discussed during readings, unless otherwise requested by the client or requested by the client or required by a court of law."

The following are examples of statements that reflect values and styles:

1. I do not foretell the future with Tarot cards, nor will I refer a client to anyone who claims they can.

2. I will respect the moral, religious and social beliefs of my clients, and will refrain from any judgment and criticism. I will adhere to the standards set forth by the ATA, including the Code of Ethics of this organization.

I have what I call my "disclaimer," to manifest informed consent when approached by a client who is expressly seeking advice from the cards. I report that *I* do not make predictions and do not tell my clients what to do with their life. Then I turn it around to describe what I will do, such as look for guidance, and support clients to discover their own answers. Of the people who come to me for a reading, 99.5% are relieved by this response, while the remaining .5% only want a prediction and appreciate that I did not waste their money or time, a sentiment that I share. I'm happy to refer people to qualified readers who work with predictions when someone makes that request.

I suggest that you visit various websites and read what other Tarot professionals have posted about their code of ethics. You may wish to develop a guideline of your own.

While the subject of ethics is vast, I have narrowed my focus on counseling ethics to issues involving the Tarot reader's level of awareness and sense of responsibility. First, I want to discuss power dynamics between client and reader, followed by a look at boundaries for each.

POWER DYNAMICS

> "The sources of healing and awareness are deep within each of us, and your task is never under any circumstances to impose your beliefs but to enable them to find these within themselves."
> — Sogyal Rimpoche *The Tibetan Book of Living and Dying*

What does the vast topic of power have to do with Tarot and reading cards? For the purpose of this discussion, it is described as responsibility for the meaning and message of the reading. For example, if a Tarot reader interprets the cards in a reading, and prescribes a particular action based on that interpretation, the power resides with the reader. Of course, the recipient of a reading has the choice of accepting that directive or not, but the authority of the reader as the oracle of the cards can weight heavily upon their choice. How a reader engages the cards and client speaks volumes about how they carry their power.

How do power dynamics appear in a Tarot reading? Often, there is an assumption that the Tarot reader is an authority in the field, and the client tends to hand over power to the reader or the reader's interpretation of the cards.

I would like to challenge all readers to consider power dynamics when working with clients. Here are some questions to ask your self:

- Do I take pride or gain esteem from reading cards for others?
- Do I routinely interpret the cards for others?
- Do I take credit for being "right" about the results of a reading?
- Do I take it personally when my predictions or projections are "wrong?"

If you answered "Yes" to any of these questions, you may want to consider the secondary benefits you gain from your work with Tarot, and whether your need for acquiring these benefits tends to override your clients' needs. For example, if a reader makes a prediction that the client will be married in the next year, and this prediction comes true, the reader might feel validated in their approach and interpretation of the original reading about marriage. But, what if this marriage was a result of the client's belief in the "rightness" of the Tarot reading, and they chose to become married in alignment with the prediction over the "rightness" of the client's choice of who to marry? This is what we may call a self-fulfilling prophecy, for had the reader exercised more restraint in making that prediction, and, instead, supported the client's unexpressed need to approach the *subject* of marriage, but with more awareness, then the possibility of an unsatisfactory result based on the marriage prediction may never occur.

Ego gratification as a secondary benefit does not support a client and can easily contaminate a reading. Putting one's subjective interpretation aside to receive more input from the client allows greater objectivity for the reader while supporting balance and personal connection for the client with the reading. Whose reading is it anyway? This relates to a subject from the last chapter, **"Following or Leading the Client in a Reading,"** which includes a classic counseling technique that Tarot professionals could benefit from incorporating into their reading style.

BOUNDARIES

Boundaries define who we are to ourselves and to others as a clear delineation of our space, be it emotional, psychic, spiritual or physical. Respecting your own as well as a client's boundary is a significant concern within the Tarot reading relationship. As already expressed, whose reading is it? By this I mean who takes responsibility for the interpretation, meaning, or outcome of the reading? I suggest that readings can be a co-creative experience for both the reader and the client, but this process requires awareness, otherwise you can unintentionally fall into a counter-transference situation. (see Chapter 4).

Within this professional relationship, various dynamics and interactions may occur. Utilizing counseling skills and awareness, the reader has more choices for how to conduct the reading when considering the following responsibilities.

The subject of boundaries includes, but is not limited to the following concepts:

- Consent – client and reader approve the conditions of their reading.
- Competence – the reader is well qualified to offer the reading.
- Privacy – the reading is offered in a secluded area.
- Confidentiality – no disclosure of the client's name or personal information by the reader.
- Dual relationships or roles – when a reader has two or more kinds of roles (family, friend, co-worker) concurrently with a client, watch for any conflict of interest.
- Conflict of interest - tainted by the possibility of favoritism or personal gain.
- Scope of practice – working within the reader's area of expertise or professional credential.
- Reader's self-disclosure – revealing information of a private nature may or may not be appropriate.
- Psychic space – honoring the client's limits on information or topics.
- Decency – moral integrity, free from obscenity.
- Physical contact – when permission is granted, within guidelines of decency.
- Meeting outside of the reading relationship – maintain awareness of potential dual roles.

Here is an example of how some of these boundary issues may appear in a reading relationship. The client is also the manager at a business where you both work (dual roles). During the reading the client reveals that there will be layoffs soon and is trying to decide who to keep and who to release (confidential information). The department where you work is one that may be released (conflict of interest). This reading could either be a profound test of the reader's objectivity, or the reader could request to be excused, followed by a referral to another competent reader.

Going back to my "disclaimer," I was modeling my boundary as a Tarot reader. It would be a violation of my personal values to enter into a predictive style of reading the cards. Notice, I claim *my* boundary rather than projecting it as my client's boundary. Predictive reading represents a boundary issue for me due to risk of it falling into a paternalistic pattern with the client by shifting the power dynamic to one of authority and child, leader and follower.

As you explore the parameters of your boundaries in reading, consider these issues:

- What are your boundaries as a reader? What will you not do in a session?
- What happens if the client has an emotional response to the reading?
- What if the client mentions someone you know, do you speak up?
- If you gave a profound reading, do you tell others of the details?
- Do you tell others who your clients are, particularly if the client is famous?

LEGAL ISSUES

Legally offering our service as Tarot professionals can be risky business at times. We have come a long way with great strides being made by valiant individuals and organizations to legitimize our field. As time goes by and more Tarot professionals challenge the old assumptions about our service and art, look to greater options being created to legitimize our work. In the mean time, to be forewarned is to be forearmed.

I'm not a lawyer or solicitor and it is beyond my scope of practice to give legal advice. However, here are some of the legal parameters I have considered as I have taught and worked with Tarot clients around the world. My recommendation is that you perform a thorough research or hire a competent lawyer or solicitor, to assist you in uncovering the specific legal requirements in your location that influence your practice.

Local laws and ordinances. Look up national as well as local government levels of laws or ordinances for your area. Here is where Tarot readers can encounter legal repercussions. I'm not trying to be a harbinger of fear for I know that service performed most ethically can transcend the politics of law … but be aware.

So what title do you use to distinguish your role or your work? Using the terms "counseling" or "counselor" could be a red flag to legal or certification authorities in your area. Some readers may use the term "consultant" to avoid being confused with mental health practitioners, but I would check for legal definitions of these terms in the governing laws to better determine what actually fits your service.

Some readers are protected by the credentials of their profession, such as certified counselors or registered spiritual authorities, but the use of Tarot reading under these professional roles can still be called into question by local, national, or global agencies. Prejudice and judgment can also work against the professional who utilizes Tarot, threatening their standing in their professional community.

"For entertainment only" is appropriate for some readers, while many Tarot professionals are offended by this label.

Mary Greer wrote an informative article titled *Fortunetelling Protected Under First Amendment*. Her weblog (marygreer.wordpress.com) posted a report on a successful "free speech" case from one of the state courts in the U.S. *The Tarosophy Tarot Town* (tarot-town.com) online social networking community recently started a campaign called "Legal Eagle" to collect information about local ordinances and Tarot. With the intension of deepening this exploration and expanding our understanding of Tarot wisdom, I created a community discussion website on the topic of *Tarot Spirituality* (TarotSpirituality.org). I extend a personal invitation to you to participate in this dynamic process.

This book has been offered with the hope of inspiring Tarot readers to raise the bar on your chosen profession or hobby, and to bring more awareness into your lives, and that of your clients. I invite you to consider and then practice some of these skills and guidelines, with legal diligence. To continue growing your knowledge and to keep current on the latest developments, there are many online resources and Tarot folks dedicated to the ongoing body of Tarot reading knowledge, skills, and ethics.

As much as I promote knowledge of ethical standards and personal boundary awareness, I believe there is an ethical dimension that includes, yet transcends these guidelines. I call it the deep ethics of compassion and love. Based on the "Metaskills" taught by Dr. Amy Mindell (presented in Chapter 4) and the spiritual wisdom of many sources, including the Tarot, cultivating a presence of attention, awareness, and love sets a tone for engaging with others that opens the door to intimacy and transformation. It cannot be taught in a mere book, but I hope to model it and live it each day.

With this in mind, sample readings are offered in the next chapter in an effort to model the mechanics and flow of the TTC approach.

6

Sample Readings

"Since the divine principles of man are obscured and latent within him, so that consciousness, of itself and by itself is unable to climb to the distant heights of spiritual intimacy with universal life, Magic in the hands of a trained and experienced Magus is the means whereby that eclipse of the inner light may be overcome."
— Israel Regardie *The Art of Magic*

I have performed thousands of Tarot readings for clients and friends, with each session being completely unique. Selecting the sample readings for this chapter has been a challenge, since some would include significant data, while others pertinent highlights. I could not possibly include everything I would like in this short book. Ultimately, I chose to create composite readings to touch upon the main points presented in the preceding chapters to support your understanding of this material.

To assist in teaching the principles of Transformative Tarot Counseling™ (TTC), I describe each sample reading with key concepts printed in *italics*.

In the spirit of *confidentiality*, names and details have been changed to respect the *privacy* of these who graciously granted *permission* to share their readings.

Card Layout for Readings

There are many types and styles of layouts for cards. When talking with clients about the issues, questions, or desires for which they wish guidance, consider what spread would be the best match. Many books have been written on this topic and I encourage you to explore and practice various approaches.

I developed my TTC layout in 1990 to better facilitate the dynamic tension and synthesis necessary for transformation and change when reading cards. An entire book can be written on the versatility of my layout. If the reader pays attention, this dynamic tension or duality appears between card positions, but can also appear within a single card, or within the client.

The TTC layout is a simple four-card spread with the following positions: 1) subject, 2) known/conscious, 3) unknown/unconscious, and 4) possible outcome/next step.

Preparation for Reading

Those of us in the *intuitive* or metaphysical consulting realm know that a reading starts long before the client arrives. Paying *attention* to subtle feelings, inner visions, and *awareness* of cues from your environment can provide information that could be related to the client you are about to see. A reader I visited years ago prayed the night before our session to help her open to divine guidance. Meditation is employed by some readers to prepare for tuning into subconscious or unconscious messages. Rituals for preparing a reading can include tools such as candles, scents, sacred objects, colors, and perhaps sounds. They can also serve as distractions, so be clear on what is essential to your work. Keeping all channels of perception open — by this I mean the interior, as well as exterior senses of sight, sound, sensation, scent, movement/vibration, and sometimes taste — supports your *awareness* and ability to perceive *intuitive cues*.

Another important consideration for the reader is providing a comfortable, *safe*, setting for the client. Is there *privacy*? Could the session be interrupted? Ideally, cell phones are turned off and doors are locked. A designated telephone line is best for phone work. Basically, do you have a *safe container* for your *alchemical* work?

I begin most of my sessions by *introducing* the client to my work style, and my *disclaimer* that I do not make predictions. I look for *guidance* to *support* the client in *discovering* their own answers. While I *introduce* myself, and my *values* to the client, I *engage* them with my *heart open* as I set the *tone* for our developing *relationship*. It is apparent that I *value* the client and am there to create *sacred* space *together* with an *ethical* and *deep presence*. Thus, querent and reader enter the first step of the *magical art* by leaping into the *unknown* together.

As I shuffle the cards, I *ask the client to talk* about the issue for which she wishes to receive *guidance*, while also blending the client's energy with the cards as I *listen*. I *explain* my process as we continue *exploring*. The most meaningful query is not always revealed at first, so I work with the client to find the question behind the question. If there is no question or issue, we are open to whatever guidance wishes to come through the reading.

Once we have gained clarity on the intended subject, we start to lay out the cards, one at a time, as in the following readings.

Sample Session #1

Mary expresses that she has "a longing to go in, to work with her inner life," but also notes her resistance due to fear of abandonment and anxiety over missing her community.

When I hear the word "abandonment", I wonder if this is a life-long pattern for the client, perhaps something from her childhood. I then make a mental note to pay attention to this possibility. If you are not a mental health professional, be sure to stay within your *scope of practice*. At the end of the reading you may consider checking in with the client to see if she has sought support for this issue or would like a *referral* to a counseling professional.

In my case, as a mental health professional I realize the block that abandonment issues can create. In an effort to bring more transparency to our process, I ask Mary, "Is it okay for me to put on my counseling hat?" This metaphor is something I use to acknowledge that this is within my *scope of practice* although it dips into a *dual role*. She responds affirmatively. I ask, "Is there a possibility that you have had abandonment issues from your past, perhaps your family of origin?" To which she immediately confirms and identifies having issues with emotional abandonment.

Why would I ask this? Mary and I are still working on the query, steeped in the *Negredo stage*, searching for the heart of her concern, so that guidance from the reading will have the greatest potential to support her in a *life-affirming* way. I'm still shuffling the cards while using my *intuitive* connection with the deck to give me an indication of when we have settled on the issue that they wish to reflect. As readers, we each have an *intuitive style* of connecting with the cards. If you don't have one yet, you will in time.

"Could the topic of abandonment be the issue we should explore?" I inquire while *watching* the client's verbal and non-verbal response, waiting for her *congruent permission*. The cards concur, so I stop shuffling. If Mary had indicated a lack of sincere willingness, I would not have approached the topic. Readers can slip into *boundary* violations if they ignore *feedback,* or negative cues, from their clients.

I go on to explain that the first card in my layout will indicate if this is the topic to focus on at this time. It could also send us in a completely different, unintended direction. This *prepares* the client for the *fluidity* of my style of working with the Tarot, which develops *communication* with the cards as they *reveal* themselves.

I invite Mary to, "Cut the cards, any way you like." This not only *engages* Mary's energy with the cards, but also starts her *intuitive* juices flowing by inviting her to *follow* her unique notion of how to cut the cards, a less *directive,* while more *creative* and *interactive* approach. Our *intuitive dance* begins as I notice if Mary stacks the cards back together as one or leaves piles for me to stack. What if the client doesn't wish to cut the cards? How a client engages the cards gives me clues that indicate the level or type of interaction each client might prefer.

As I'm turning the first card over, I ask Mary, "What is your first impression of this card? I invite you to notice what catches you attention in the card—a feeling or reaction, an association or whatever comes up for you—and please let me know." In consideration of my own *boundary,* I tell Mary to feel free to touch the card. Practicing *beginner's mind,* I'm as excited about the prospect of what may arise as my client is feeling.

When Mary's card is visible, she reports seeing "Quan Yin". With *curiosity* I ask her to tell me more about her understanding of Quan Yin. Even though I know this goddess well, it is more important to *listen* to Mary's *description* very carefully, since it may be a *mirror* of her central theme or archetypal lesson. She responds, "Softness, love, understanding."

Notice that I neither mention the name of the card, nor offer an *interpretation* of its meaning. In fact, I'm not adding anything other than repeating her exact words, as I *mirror* back to Mary her *perceptions*. This *grounds* her *impression*, graces her with undivided *attention*, and leaves the reading *open* for more *intuitive connections*.

To further *anchor* this *awareness* in Mary, I ask her, "Can you *embody* the *essence* of Quan Yin and *experience* softness, love and understanding within you?" She becomes very quiet, closes her eyes, and gives herself a minute to *actualize* this energy within herself. I *notice* a peaceful expression upon her face with gentle breathing, much different from her anxious demeanor when the topic of abandonment first appeared.

From a counseling perspective, I could spend the rest of the session reinforcing this new awareness for Mary knowing it has healing energy for her. But...this is a Tarot session. *Honoring* the original intention for the session, of conducting a Tarot reading, is important. It preserves our *safe container*, as does *completing* the session within the agreed upon *time*.

Next, Mary notices a "meteor shower" in the card and gets more excited, as she makes an association with a dream she had the night before. The more she views this scene in the card, the more she recognizes aspects of her dream, as if it is coming to life. She tunes into the flowing nature, the movement of the shower.

To facilitate a connection between the original issue and the querent's personal experience of the card, I ask Mary, "From Quan Yin's point of view, does the reading want to explore your desire to turn your attention inward, and maybe, reexamine abandonment issues?" To which she responds, "She is supportive and unconditional, there is no judgment from her as she says to do what you need to do."

We *combine* Mary's *intuitive* information with the *feeling-tone inspired* by the card to uncover *personal* meaning for her. As the reader, the *Magus*, I begin to *blend* the client's *insights* with mine, then add my knowledge of the card and the role of it's layout position.

Quan Yin is the central goddess on XVII The Star card in my *Voyager Tarot* deck. My *intuition* guides me to *share* her message of compassion for Mary, to look for clarity within, while being quiet without, and to be tranquil in her contemplation. This serves as a *confirmation* of her chosen subject for the reading. Mary *resonates* with this summary. Please note, there can be varying interpretations of the same Tarot trump, so I stay close to the essence of it's message while utilizing descriptions that resonate more closely with the client's intuitive impression.

Now we are ready to move onto the next card, occupying the position of the "known" or "*conscious awareness*" in my TTC layout. I *prepare* the client for this step of the reading by *describing* the second position as representing something she already *recognizes* about herself in this issue.

Once the second card is revealed, Mary makes a slight shrill as she notices an iris flower and *associates* it with her mother, because it was her favorite flower. She adds that her mother is recently deceased. Her gaze moves to another flower and describes that it is blossoming, much like she is experiencing at this time of her life. Mary *tracks* a theme from her previously mentioned dream, as she *identifies* with the flowing *energy* of the cards. Her experience of this card sends a message *directly* to her, to "stay in the flow" of things in her life.

I *draw* Mary's attention to the title of this *Voyager* card, "Surfer," as we both laugh about her being this surfer on the ocean of her e-motions, energy in motion. This is the Man of Cups card, associated with the Knight of Cups in other decks, and he encourages the querent to take action and be more fluid in her emotional expression.

Mary admits that she has been actively working on grieving the loss of her mother. She can see how this energy in her life is the motivation for her to push herself to explore her emotional material more clearly. This awareness is well *grounded* in the client, so we move onto the third card.

I report to Mary that the third card is here to help or guide her to the next step of her *process*. This card position is called the unknown, meaning that it is not fully conscious or identified with at this time. When you are reading for clients, please try to be mindful that unidentified aspects of *Self* can be *shadow* material…our greatest potential…or most challenging block.

"Nefertiti is what I see…the Egyptian queen!!" exclaims Mary with a childlike glee, with her rhyming voice as *expressive* as her hands while her arms take flight. I imitate the movement of her arms and *reflect* back to her the enthusiasm of her tone, which she instantly *identifies* as the theme of flowing that runs through the reading. Blooming, expansion, stretching are *experienced* by Mary more *deeply* and *personally*.

When I mention the name of this third card, III The Empress, the *archetypal* mother of the Tarot, the client immediately *associates* it with the unfinished grieving process over her deceased mother. *Connections* begin to be made between the client's old perception of being emotionally abandoned (fear/contraction) and her newfound opportunity to mother herself with the unconditional love of her inner Empress (love/expansion). Excitement and *tears* appear as Mary *embraces* this *realization*.

Now we begin to see the deeper theme of the original issue, as progressively *unveiled* in the reading. Mary's desire to go inside was blocked by her fear of abandonment. The cards and her *intuition* now reveal that she can heal old issues with her mother, by removing the projection of unmet love from her mother and then *transforming* the source of love to her inner life, to re-mother herself with unconditional love.

"III Empress" *Voyager Tarot* by James Wanless

Mary moves very quickly through her reading because she is already engaged in her *individuation* process. Mary happens to be a counseling professional who is well versed in the process of healing. She understands the dance that leads to a *synergistic blending* of these two *contrasting* energies. Another client might need more time and *patience* to reach greater levels of *awareness*. That is where the reader's *skills* come into play as the sacred *midwife* to help the client birth new possibilities. If the reading ends with a sense that the client needs more support to resolve issues that may have surfaced, be prepared to make suggestions for *referrals*.

To further *ground* the reading's revealed message, I end the session by summarizing Mary's *journey* through the cards — the essence of her story of *self-discovery* and coming home to her heart.

Sample Session #2

Jack is a widower who recently retired from a successful career and is in search of meaning in his later years. He begins the reading with two questions, one about his health and the other his new role in his community.

Health, legal, and similar questions that are out of my *scope of practice* are discouraged. So I state my *disclaimer*...that I will not make predictions or tell him what to do with his life. He acknowledges my *boundary* and agrees to continue with the reading.

Initially, Jack shows stronger *feelings* about his standing in the community. I wish to *draw* him out so I ask, "Can you say more about that?"

Jack expresses a desire to be of service to his community, but worries about the factions in his locale and does not believe he fits into any one group. Thinking there might be more options in a larger community, he ponders whether he should stay in the area or relocate. Jack expresses he does not know how to move forward with his intent and purpose in life at this time of transition.

I ask Jack, "Could you go ahead and state your intent and purpose?" He responds that it is a spiritual calling. However, this remains vague. We continue to explore and "*tease out*" the issue. He comes to realize that he is torn between his concern for his physical wellness and his identity as a spiritual being.

It is time to cut the cards and turn the first one over. As he views the card, Jack makes several interesting *sounds*, which I mirror with *blank access* utterances like…"hmm." He notices the card title, The Lovers, but sadly expresses the couple in the card are split. He gets a little choked up with *emotions* as he reminisces about his wife and how she cared for him. Jack says he now has to assume both roles, as the caregiver and the one who needs care, but that he still feels alone now that his wife has passed on.

Jack next sees the lovers' arms embracing and he *imagines* being held by arms. He *relates* to a message of oneness in the card. At this point I sum up the subject of the reading by reviewing Jack's process and reporting my observation. "First you see separateness in things, then you realize how they are being held together. So could the reading be about how to shift your perceptions to see the connections more clearly and immediately?"

Jack begins to see this *theme* in other areas of the *Voyager* Lovers card, noticing a spiritual side—the "heavens" where there is light, joy and love, contrasted by a dark side, the "dark night of his soul." Yet they are both there, together. I *add* that on a spiritual level, this card is about embracing his own lightness and darkness, as the inner lovers.

Looking at the second card, Jack comments that there is a lot of darkness, and admits he may be letting the darkness overshadow things in his life. I *concur*, as I *tie* that message in with card *knowledge* about the Five of Crystals (Swords), saying that the crystal clarity of his mind is challenged by the swords' ego attachments and mental perceptions. He *relates* this back to his pattern of falling into fear whenever met with a challenge. This acknowledgement helps him *recognize* how negativity comes into play in his life. Jack has now *grounded* the *known* placement position in his spread, more aware now of how he has blocked his own ability to feel connected with life by entertaining feelings of fear.

He is eager for the guidance of the upcoming third card, seeking more balance in his current situation. While viewing the new card Jack expresses, "That's a nice card." To which I ask with *curiosity*, "What is nice about it?" He further describes, "It's light… and the darkness is way in the back." This shift in focus has a lot of meaning for Jack, bringing the light to the front. The negativity isn't gone, but has faded far into the background. Jack elaborates, "I see earth light, but things are running down from the heavens as well which gives me some positive thoughts."

To invite more awareness on the *dance of opposites* between the last two cards, I *inquire*, "How did you get from the darkness of the second card to bringing more light into the foreground of the third card?" Jack immediately responds, "Let go and let God!"

It is time to bring in Tarot *knowledge* to *support* the client's *realization*. So I talk about this third card, the Nine of Crystals (Swords), and its role in letting go of old perceptions, removing the distractions of ego attachments by finding ones Hermit-like inner source of light — his deep inner knowing.

We talk about not losing touch with one's inner light, even in the darkest moments. Jack *realizes* that he has stayed in the same community because he has a quiet home, inspired by nature to feel close to God. "My spirit family walks with me here."

In order to be *thorough*, I go back to topics we touched upon in our *process*, and ask what the reading is saying about where Jack should live. He answers, "I'm here as long as I need to be, but it is not where I will be eventually." I *add* that the Hermit, associated with the number nine, shines his spiritual light wherever he goes.

Next we go back to the health question, and Jack receives this message from his cards, "You're worrying too much." What he begins to realize is that the negativity of his thoughts is what creates his worries. Being alone has left him with his thoughts, thus he is worrying more than before. He *realizes* his health issue is more worry than it is real. To back this up, I *confirm* that Jack has medical *professionals* with whom he can *consult*.

Jack's reading has one final card, the Two of Crystals (Swords), which to him represents mental balance and insight, a beautiful summary for the guidance he sought with this reading.

I *review* the *story* in Jack's reading for him by starting with the lovers who first appeared split but were actually held in an embrace. This is the subject and the process of his reading, for what appears to be separate transforms into a united oneness.

Jack's other three cards are all crystals/swords cards, which indicated that his journey is one of identifying and shifting his perceptions—the way he sees himself and his life. The appearance of darkness associated with his fear and negativity emerged in the second card, then the third card revealed Jack's own light in the foreground. The dance between the second and the third card inspired him to embrace his own light and dark *Self*. Jack realizes he has dominion over his perceptions, such as his fear about his health, and can now see he has perpetuated his own negativity. His final card is a mirror of his work, a symbol of balance that he *experiences* with relief, hope, and a deeper sense of peace.

I did not repeat the names of the cards in the summary of Jack's reading for the following reason. I find that interpretations of cards do not matter as much as the querent's relationship to them as they develop their personalized message. I was reinforcing Jack's *impressions* of his cards. It was his *experience* of the reading that will last and inspire his life more than any words or thoughts I may have shared.

"VI Lovers" *Voyager Tarot* by James Wanless

Summary

In TTC readings, the key is to *follow* the client's *process,* then *support* them with additional *knowledge* and wisdom. If you allow the *space* and have the *patience* to *guide* your sessions, a client will find their own answers, increasing the possibility for real *change* in their life.

Transformation and *change* is the potential of each reading. I'd like to review the *magical stages* in simple terms as they appear on several levels of a session.

TRANSFORMATIVE TAROT COUNSELING READING PROCESS

A. Exploring one card at a time, each time the new card is turned over, try approaching the meaning or message of the card in the following sequence:
1. *Encourage* and *follow* the *intuition* of the querent, the "first impression."
2. Pay *attention* to your *intuition* as the reader.
3. Add your *knowledge* of the card and its relationship to its placement in the layout.
4. *Blend* all three of these steps together — the client's intuition with the reader's intuition and card knowledge — in a way that *supports* the querent's *perceptions*. Keep in mind that the final interpretation of the reading may have nothing to do with your educated *knowledge* of the cards.

B. *Build* the *relationship* between cards and positions as you move through the spread, one card at a time, until all is *revealed*:
1. *Focus* on only one card at a time to develop a *personal relationship* between the card and querent.

2. Once individual cards are *grounded* in the querent, take that *awareness* to the next level by *exploring* the *relationship* between card positions in that reading.

- For example, once the first two cards are *revealed* individually, create *relationship* with those two before moving to the third card. After the third card is *realized*, bring in the second card's energy to *explore* their *synergy*. Understanding builds with each card.
- When *polarities* or *contrasts* between cards *emerge*, go as *deeply* into the *dance* between these two as *allowed* by the client. For advanced students of counseling skills, keep in mind that the polarity may show up more strongly in the client than in the cards themselves.
- Remember the *process* of *thesis, antithesis, and synthesis* as you build toward the new message or guidance of the reading.

7

Tarot is a Powerful Tool

"The Tarot Arcana visually represent the unity of God, World, and Human. Through these images of unification one can thus *divine* the meaning of life and the direction of truth at any given time."
  — Dai Deon *Origins of the Tarot*

Some study Tarot as a book of wisdom, not just an oracle of prediction. Within its structure and symbols are a wealth of knowledge and guidance about life and life's journey. In her small but powerful book, *Inner Pathways to the Divine*, Diane Toland proclaims, "Relegating the tarot cards to the role of fortune-telling is like using a samurai sword to make a sandwich."

For years I've studied and written about what I call "The Sacred Journey of the Soul" and what the Tarot teaches about this path we all walk. In essence, it is the alpha and omega, source and return to source, trump 0 The Fool to XXI The World, with what I call the "Dance of Duality" in-between. Other fine authors, such as Hajo Banzhaf in his beautifully illustrated book, *Tarot and the Journey of the Hero,* tell a version of this story that runs through the major arcana of the Tarot.

Over the centuries, fortune-telling, prediction-making, soothsaying, and gambling have been a part of various oracular traditions. Concurrently, philosophical and spiritual wisdom were integrated into the symbolism of Tarot cards, and are still present today. There are several excellent books on the history of Tarot. My favorite book reflecting the spiritual journey and core of Tarot is *Origins of the Tarot,* by Dai Leon. I highly recommend this book to all students of Tarot wisdom. For an abbreviated and colorfully symbolic version of the history and influences on modern Tarot decks, see my *Tarot History Poster,* available to order on my website: TarotCounseling.org

There is so much more I would like to write about this topic, but must leave that for a future project.

For the purpose of this booklet there are two important points for Tarot readers, in light of what Tarot teaches us about life's journey. First, life is a process of soul development where each card or stage of one's journey is to be learned, integrated, and transcended. Second, the ultimate goal is to realize that duality is merely a tool for reflection with the purpose of raising one's soul awareness to reunite with source.

Care of the Psyche, the Soul

The next question is... how can awareness of spiritual development be applied to a reading? Tarot teaches that our spiritual evolution is an ongoing process. Following are some practical examples for supporting clients to realize the next step in their journey.

In natural, or holistic health, practitioners prefer to address the *cause* of an issue, not just the *symptom*. As a health example, a patient arrives and requests pain medication for a sore lower back. After some inquiring the health practitioner learns that this physically strong patient works in a warehouse lifting heavy boxes, but bends from the waist instead of bending at the knees while keeping the spine erect and aligned. The health practitioner might recommend that the patient receive physical therapy and learn how to efficiently lift heavy objects.

Now, if a Tarot client comes to a reading with the wish of learning whether her, or his, love interest will stay in their relationship or leave like the last one, the door is already open to explore a pattern for the client. Instead of seeking a yes or no answer about the predicted longevity of the current relationship, the deeper question in the background is the cause of the client's doubt. Some avenues of exploration could include whether there is a history of lost love or a tendency to doubt in the client's life. Another perspective that could arise in exploring the client's attachment to relationship might be whether the client's soul prefers to be in a primary relationship, or something completely different. This could lead to a very enlightening and confirming reading for the client, about prioritizing their interests and goals before investing energy in a primary relationship. In this case, minimizing the client's personal needs could be the *cause* in the background that creates the pattern, or *symptom*, of relationships ending.

The Tarot reader has the potential of setting the stage for new doors of perception to open for the client. Tarot, as a visual book of wisdom, has the purpose of inspiring each and all of us to journey toward enlightenment, to embrace a personal awareness of wholeness. Why stop at the door when we are invited to move beyond the veil? To do this requires a willingness to drop what we know and step into the unknown until it becomes familiar. When reading for another, this means going into the unknown with the client and just sitting with them, holding sacred space until they find their own way, their own light.

Dualistic Beliefs

We live in a dualist world of right and wrong, good and bad, us versus them. The Tarot teaches us how to balance these extremes, find our center, integrate our "shadow" and ultimately unite with all. Isn't that what trump XXI The World symbolizes, our triumphant return to source?

I invite readers to embrace these Tarot values as well, to move away from seeing a card as good or bad, or a reading as right or wrong. Be willing to compassionately invite the shadow in with the light, to see wholeness. Once these values are realized, the deeper essential power of Tarot as a model of our immortal journey will be more apparent, and our readings will support this potential for others.

Importance of Increasing the Quality of Our Art

Tarot reading is becoming more mainstream and accessible. As our art increases in visibility, it is paramount that we raise the standards and excellence of our service.

As a teacher and writer, I'm dedicated to raising the quality of readings offered by Tarot professionals. To this end, I have suggested counseling skills, based on my training and experience, which could enhance the feeling and effectiveness of a Tarot reading for the reader and client alike. I invite you to explore and incorporate the ideas presented in this work that best compliment your reading style. May love and light be with you.

Bibliography and Resources

Bibliography

Banzhaf, Hajo. *Tarot and the Journey of the Hero* (Samuel Weiser, 2000)

Campbell, Joseph. *The Hero With a Thousand Faces* (Pantheon Books, 1949)

— *The Power of Myth with Bill Moyers* (Doubleday, 1988)

Fabricius, Johannes. *Alchemy - The Medieval Alchemists and their Royal Art* (London: Diamond Books, 1976)

Greer, Mary. *21 Ways to Read a Tarot Card* (Llewellyn Worldwide, 2006)

Jette, Christine. *Professional Tarot: The Business of Reading, Consulting & Teaching* (Llewellyn Worldwide, 2003)

Jung, Carl. *Civilization in Transition* (Princeton University Press, 1967)

— *Alchemical Studies* (Princeton University Press, 1983)

Klossowski de Rola, Stanislas. *Alchemy - The Secret Art* (Thames and Hudson Ltd., 1973)

Kryder, Rowena Pattee. *Source - Visionary Interpretations of Global Creation Myths* (Crestone, CO: Golden Point, 2000)

Leon, Dai. *Origins of the Tarot: Cosmic Evolution and the Principles of Immortality* (Berkeley: Frog Books, 2009)

Mindell, Amy, Ph.D. *Metaskills: The Spiritual Art of Therapy* (Tempe, AZ: New Falcon Publications, 1995)

Mindell, Arnold, Ph.D. *Dreaming While Awake* (Hampton Roads, 2000)

Nichols, Sallie *Jung and Tarot: An Archetypal Journey* (Weiser, 1980)

Place, Robert M. & Guiley, Rosemary Ellen. *The Alchemical Tarot* (San Francisco, CA: Thorsons, 1995)

Regardie, Israel. *The Art and Meaning of Magic* (Helios Books, 1969)

Semetsky, Inna. *Re-Symbolization of the Self: Human Development and Tarot Hermeneutic* (Rotterdam, The Netherlands: Sense Publishers, 2011)

Toland, Diane. *Inner Pathways to the Divine* (Hygiene, CO: SunShine Press Publications, 2001)

Wanless, James. *Voyager Tarot: The Way of the Oracle* (Carmel, CA: Merrill-West Publishing, 1989)

Webster's New Universal Unabridged Dictionary (Barnes & Noble, 2003)

Weinstein, Marion. *Positive Magic: Occult Self-Help* (Custer, WA: Phoenix Publishing, 1981)

Williamson, Marianne. *A Return to Love: Reflections on the Principles of 'A Course on Miracles'* (New York: HarperPaperbacks, 1996)

Wynne, Katrina, M.A. *My Tarot Journey* (Yachats, OR: Sacred Rose Publishing, 2005)
    — *Tarot History: Poster & Chart* (Yachats, OR: Sacred Rose Publishing, 2009)

Zweig, Connie & Abrams, Jeremiah, editors. *Meeting the Shadow: The Hidden Power of the Dark Side of Human Nature* (Jeremy P. Tarcher, 1991)

Resources

This is a list of a few of my favorite Tarot and other writers. Some of them come are from a counseling or psychology background and bring that perspective to their work. Included are additional resources from my work.

Hajo Banzhaf
      www.tarotpedia.com/wiki/Banzhaf,_Hajo

Mary Greer	marygreer.wordpress.com
Rowena Pattee Kryder	www.creative-harmonics.org
Dai Leon	originsofthetarot.com
Arnold and Amy Mindell	www.aamindell.net
Robert M. Place	thealchemicalegg.com
Rachel Pollack	www.rachelpollack.com
James Ricklef	www.jamesricklef.com
James Wells	jameswells.wordpress.com
Authur Rosengarten	artrosengarten.wordpress.com
James Wanless	www.voyagertarot.com
Katrina Wynne	TarotCounseling.org
	TarotSpirituality.org
	MySacredJourney.org ~ weblog

Visit my website for links to a variety of Tarot resources: TarotCounseling.org

"Friend" me on Facebook at "Katrina Wynne" or join the "Transformative Tarot Counseling™" community page.

About the Author

A *Forest Mystic* who resides in the Pacific Northwest, **Katrina Wynne** enjoys her deep relationship with the Tarot along with caretaking the woods, tending her garden, and contemplating the universe.

Katrina has enjoyed 40 years as a mostly self-taught Tarot devotee, much of this time spent developing her unique style of working with the cards, bringing their message to life, and sharing the wonder of their wisdom with others.

Katrina's 24 years of education and training in psychotherapeutic modalities has influenced the way she works with and teaches Tarot. Her knowledge draws from mentors such as Drs. Arnold and Amy Mindell and their ongoing development of "Process Work" psychology.

Offering her expertise and service has been a calling for Katrina, including the writing of this book and several other publications. Spirit moves through her and guilds her, especially by means of the requests she receives to teach workshops and consult with Tarot clients. It was by the suggestion of her many students that she came to establish the *Transformative Tarot Counseling*™ *Certification Program* where she passes on the wisdom of her experience to others.

For more information about Katrina Wynne, M.A. and the many gifts she has to offer, please contact her through her website:

TarotCounseling.org